Contents

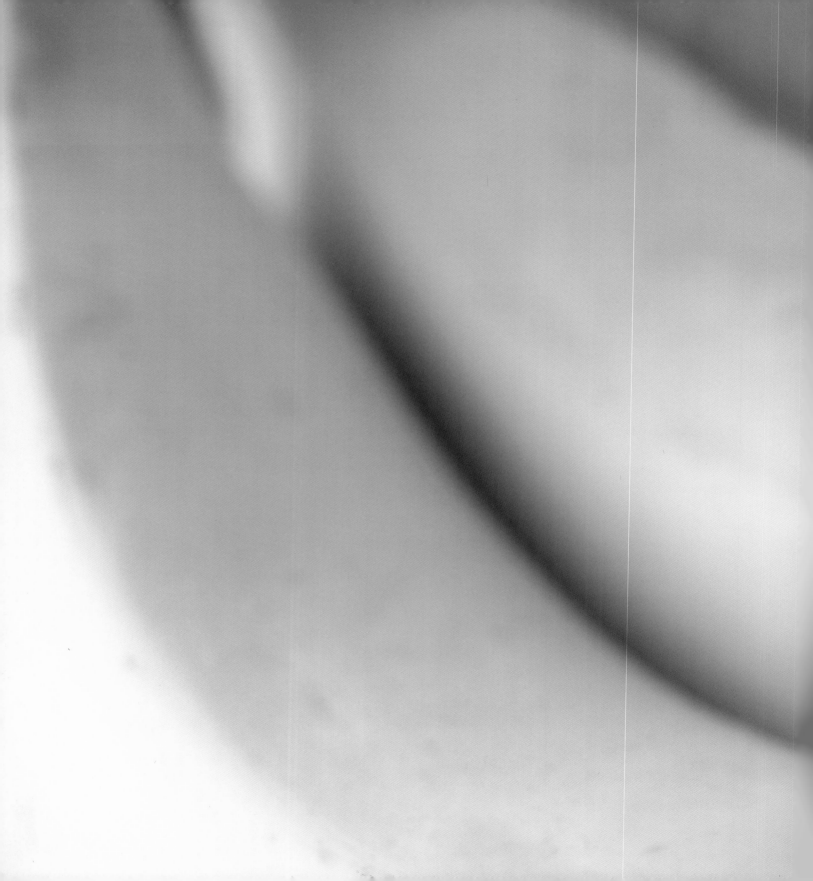

Acknowledgements

I would like to thank:

Pilar Busquet, Janice Groves, Julie Lee, Eva Stone, John Bell, Jackie Basset, George Morris, Patricia Xavier, Michelle Assimon, Pooma Devi Nadarajah, the late Mrs T Nadarajah, Lau Siew Kheng, Mdm Poon Choi Peng, Judy Tsang, Yvonne Teo, Georgina Tan and Mdm Mary Durai for sharing their family recipes with me.

Raka Metra and Ursula Vogler who tried and tested my recipes.

My family—Elitha, Eliya and Nachii—for their time, patience and support, and for tasting my fruit creations.

Introduction

"Give me books, fruit, French wine and fine weather and a little music out of doors, played by someone I do not know."

— John Keats, poet

Fruit is widely consumed for a variety of reasons. It is delicious, a rich source of vitamins and nutrients and known to have medicinal and healing properties. An orange, for example is a good source of vitamin C, potassium, folate and fibre. The best way to enjoy a fruit's colour, texture and nutritional value is to eat it in its fresh, natural state.

With a greater variety of fruit becoming widely and easily available, modern uses of fruit in cooking have created very imaginative dishes. Fruit is used, as main ingredients or accompaniments, in dishes from mains to soups, curries, preserves, sauces, sambals, chutneys, pickles to jam and marmalade. The possibilities are endless, limited only by one's imagination.

Cooking with fruit is not new. Almost every country has its special and distinctive fruit dishes. The English are proud of their apple pies and the Northern Sri Lankans have their mango sothi or soup. The Indians relish fruit sambals, pickles, chutneys and lemon rice while the Persians, Chinese and Germans use fruit in preparing their sauces.

My favourite activities include pickling fruit and making chutneys. I would take the time and spend an entire day making pickles and chutneys, especially when mangoes are in season—this is when the fruit is at its best, abundant and cheap. The distinctive fruit flavours can enhance any meal and can make eating the same dish seem like a completely new experience each time. Try making a mango chutney at home and serve it with fish or chicken, or a plum sauce and serve it as a dip for deep-fried shrimps. I assure you that the end result will be thoroughly rewarding.

This book is my personal collection of fruit recipes that will whet your appetite. The recipes have been collected from various countries where I have travelled to and tasted these dishes. I am sure their delicious and unique flavours will be a welcome change to those of you who are looking for something different from your usual home fare.

Happy Cooking!

N. Maheswari Devi

Selecting and Handling Fruit

When choosing fruit, always select fruit that is in season as it will be at its prime and sweetest. Select fresh, vibrant-coloured fruit and avoid fruit with blemishes, scars, bruises or any other visible evidence of decay. As a general rule, the fruit should feel relatively heavy and firm. Dull-looking and soft fruit would usually indicate that it is overripe.

Fruit is highly perishable so proper storage is important. Only wash fruit just before using as excess moisture encourages spoilage. Store ripe fruit in the refrigerator. Unripe fruit left at room temperature will ripen in 3 to 5 days. There are many ways to ripen fruit. They usually involve either increasing the temperature of the environment of the fruit or storing the fruit in paper bags, a method that works well with fruit such as apricots, nectarines and peaches.

Fruit can be preserved through freezing, drying, canning, pickling or making jams. When storing jams, fruit purées and juices, always leave a 2.5-cm (1-in) space between the jam and the lid of the container so that the lids are unaffected by food acid, otherwise they may corrode and allow air to enter. When freezing fruit, cut fruit into smaller chunks before storing in plastic containers. Fruit such as melons, berries, mangoes and grapes freeze well, but others such as tomatoes and oranges do not because of their high water content, which makes them vulnerable to ice-crystal damage. When using frozen fruit, leave to thaw in the unopened container at room temperature for 3 to 4 hours or leave to thaw out slowly overnight in the fridge before using or consuming.

1   Bananas   7   Nectarines
2   Watermelon   8   Green mangoes
3   Grapefruit   9   Oranges
4   Tomato   10   Mandarin orange
5   Lemon   11   Pear
6   Peaches

12

26

24

23

25

Fruit Glossary

Name	Description
Apple (*Malies communis*)	An apple is round and has a distinct crown. This fruit has yellow, green or red skin and a sweet to tart taste. Choose firm, average-sized apples and store in the refrigerator.
Avocado (*Persea americana*)	This pear-shaped fruit has a thin green skin that turns black when ripe. The flesh is nutty flavoured and creamy in texture. Buy avocados when they are green and leave them to ripen at room temperature.
Banana (*Musa paradisiaca*)	The banana is native to Southeast Asia but is now cultivated all over the world. It is green when unripe and yellow when ripe. It is commonly used in desserts and can be used in curries.
Cherry (*Prunus avium*)	The cherry is native to Eastern Europe and Western Asia. It is eaten raw, or made into jams and used in pies. Choose cherries that are firm-fleshed, shiny, unblemished and brightly coloured.
Coconut (*Cocos nucifera*)	The coconut has a shell, seed and cavity. The shell is hard, thick and brown. The white flesh that makes up the seed is edible and the liquid that fills the cavity is known as coconut water. This is not to be confused with coconut cream or milk, which is obtained through the process of grating and squeezing the white coconut flesh.
Dates (*Phoenix dactylifera*)	This oval-shaped fruit has brown skin and soft and sweet flesh. Dates have a high sugar content. Good quality dates are plump, glossy and have slightly wrinkled skin. When selecting dates, avoid dates that are cracked or broken. Dates are often used in stuffings and salads.

Grapes *(Vitis vinifera)*	Grapes grow in clusters and come in a variety of colours: green, blue and purple-red. Keep grapes in a clean plastic bag, in the crisp section of the refrigerator. Grapes will store for up to 1 week. Raisins are dried grapes that are either sun-dried or oven-dried. Dark raisins are sweet while golden raisins are tangy in taste. Raisins are often used in salads, cookies, breads and cakes.
Grapefruit *(Citrus paradisi)*	This large, round, yellow-skinned fruit has juicy acidic pulps that are either white or pink. Select grapefruits that are firm, heavy and shiny.
Lemon *(Citrus limon)*	This yellow-skinned fruit has a high vitamin content. Its refreshing flavour makes it popular in drinks, sauces and salad dressings. Look for smooth-skinned lemons that feel heavy as these are the juiciest. Surface marks rarely affect the taste of the fruit.
Lime *(Citrus aurantifolia)*	This small, oval citrus fruit has thin green skin and juicy pale green pulp. Look for firm, smooth-skinned limes that feel heavy as they are the juiciest.
Mangoes *(Mangifera indica)*	The original name of this fruit comes from the Tamil word *man-kai*. The fruit has a large stone and varies in size and shape. Mangoes ripen in a variety of colours such as yellow, orange and red. Ripe mangoes have a fruity aroma and juicy flesh. Unripe mangoes or green mangoes are green with pale flesh that is crisp and tart. Green mangoes are used in salads or are simply eaten on their own, or with salt or sugar.

Orange *(Citrus sinensis)*	Orange is the generic name for fruits of the citrus tree. The common orange is round, orange-skinned and has a sweet and juicy pulp. Another common variety of oranges, known as mandarin, clementine or tangerine, has a thin skin that peels easily and is slightly flatter in shape than the common orange.
Papaya *(Carica papaya)*	Also known as paw-paw, papayas come in a range of sizes from small to large. When ripe, the skins of papayas turn yellow. A ripe papaya has melon-like flesh that is orange in colour, soft and sweet. Use papayas in fruit salads and desserts.
Passion fruit *(Passiflora)*	This round fruit has either yellow or dark purple skin and contains edible black seeds that are covered with a yellow jelly-like flesh. Passion fruit is an excellent source of Vitamin C and dietary fibre. Select passion fruit that have smooth and slighty wrinkled skin. The passion fruit is commonly used in sorbets, sauces and drinks.
Peach *(Prunus persica)*	Native to China, the peach is sometimes called the "Queen of Fruit". It has a soft, fuzzy surface, a single stone and either white or yellow flesh. Select peaches that are fragrant, firm and deep-coloured. Their sweet flesh makes them a suitable dessert fruit. Peaches can be bought both canned or fresh.
Pears *(Pyrus communis)*	Pears come in a variety of shapes, from bell-shaped to round. Its fragrant, buttery, sweet and juicy flesh can be added into salads or cooked as a dessert. Pears are also a good accompaniment to poultry.
Pineapple *(Ananas comosus)*	Native to South America, the pineapple has a distinct reddish and golden skin. Its yellow-coloured flesh is sweet and acidic and is suitable for cooking with meats. Select pineapples that are fragrant, firm and plump.
Plum *(Prunus)*	Plums are the second most cultivated fruit in the world. This smooth-skinned fruit is a member of the rose family. Its skin colour ranges from red to black. Select plums that have smooth, unblemished and bright-coloured skins. When ripe, plums will have a faint fragrance and will be soft to the touch. Although plums are also known as prunes in France, the term prunes is usually used with reference to dried plums.

Pomegranate *(Punica granatum)*	Native to Asia, the pomegranate has a smooth leathery skin and contains small red seeds. The edible seeds are translucent, ruby-coloured, juicy and crunchy. Add pomegranate seeds to dishes for flavour and texture or juice them to enjoy their natural sweet and tart taste.
Nectarine *(Prunus persicavar nectarina)*	This medium-sized fruit is similar to the peach. What distinguishes a nectarine from a peach is its smooth and rich yellow-red coloured skin. Select nectarines that are firm and shiny.
Strawberry *(Fragaria virginiana)*	This plump, bright red-coloured berry is a rich source of Vitamin C and fibre. Select strawberries that are dry, firm, plump and evenly-coloured. Strawberries are available fresh or frozen.
Tomato *(Lycopersicon esculentum)*	Native to South America, the tomato comes in a number of varieties. The most commonly available tomatoes are the plum tomato, cherry tomato and beefsteak tomato. When choosing tomatoes, avoid those with cuts, bruises or blemishes. Select tomatoes that are firm and have smooth and rich-coloured skins. Add raw tomatoes to salads, meat stews or curries.
Watermelon *(Citrullus lanatus)*	A member of the cucumber family, watermelons range in size from small to very large. This fruit has a thick green skin and a juicy yellow or red-coloured flesh. Select watermelons that are firm, smooth and heavy.

SOUPS

"Soup puts the heart at ease, calms down the violence of hunger,
eliminates the tension of the day, and awakens and refines the appetite."

Augueste Escoffier

Spicy Tomato Rasam   22

Lime Juice Rasam   25

Lamb Soup with Tomato   26

Jamaican Avocado Soup   29

Lemony Lamb Soup   30

Tomato Orange Soup   33

Apricot Lentil Soup   34

Mango Soup   36

SPICY TOMATO RASAM

Serves 6–8

Ingredients

Tamarind pulp	60 g (2 oz)
Red lentils	60 g (2 oz)
Ground turmeric	$1/4$ tsp
Tomatoes	4, large, finely chopped
Garlic	2 cloves, peeled and crushed
Chilli powder	$1/2$ tsp
Cumin seeds	1 tsp
Asafoetida	a pinch
Black peppercorns	$1/2$ tsp
Salt	to taste
Cooking oil	1 Tbsp
Mustard seeds	$1/2$ tsp
Curry leaves	a handful
Dried chillies	2, chopped

Method

- Steep tamarind in 250 ml (8 fl oz / 1 cup) boiling water for 15–20 minutes. Strain and reserve liquid.

- Put lentils, turmeric and 1.5 litres (48 fl oz / 6 cups) water in a pot. Bring to the boil and simmer for 20 minutes, or until lentils are soft.

- Add tomatoes, garlic, chilli powder, cumin, asafoetida, peppercorns, salt to taste and tamarind liquid. Cook for another 10 minutes over medium heat.

- Heat oil in a frying pan. Add mustard seeds, curry leaves and dried chillies. When mustard seeds splutter, pour contents into the pot. Bring to the boil for 2–3 minutes. Ladle soup into serving bowls and serve hot.

LIME JUICE RASAM

Serves 3–4

Ingredients

Water	500 ml (16 fl oz / 2 cups)
Yellow split lentils	90 g (3 oz), soaked and drained
Garlic (optional)	2 cloves, peeled and crushed
Ground turmeric	$1/2$ tsp
Cooking oil	4 tsp
Mustard seeds	$1/4$ tsp
Dried chilli (optional)	1, halved
Lime juice	75 ml ($2^1/2$ fl oz / 5 Tbsp)

Masala

Chilli powder	1 tsp
Ground cumin	$1/2$ tsp
Black peppercorns	12, crushed
Coriander leaves (cilantro)	1 sprig
Salt	to taste

Method

- Bring water to the boil. Add lentils, garlic, if desired, turmeric and 1 tsp oil. Return to the boil, reduce heat and simmer for 25 minutes, or until soft. Remove from heat.

- Using a wooden spoon, mash lentils in the pot until mixture has the consistency of thick soup.

- Add all masala ingredients to mashed lentils and mix well.

- Return pot to heat. Add enough water to make about 1 litre (32 fl oz / 4 cups) *rasam*, stir and bring to the boil. Remove from heat.

- Heat remaining oil in a frying pan. Add mustard seeds and dried chilli, if desired, and when seeds splutter, add to *rasam*.

- Stir in lime juice and mix well. Ladle into bowls and serve either hot or cold.

LAMB SOUP WITH TOMATO

Serves 4–5

Ingredients

Lamb shoulder	150 g (5 oz), thinly sliced
Ground black pepper	to taste
Light soy sauce	1 Tbsp
Cooking oil	1 Tbsp
Onion	1, peeled and thinly sliced
Red chilli	1, cut into 3 pieces
Tomato	1, quartered
Lamb stock	1 litre (32 fl oz / 4 cups) (see pg 151)
Salt	to taste

Method

- Rub lamb with pepper and soy sauce and set aside to marinate for 20 minutes.

- Heat oil in a nonstick saucepan over medium heat. When very hot, add onion, chilli and tomato. Fry for 1 minute, stirring continuously.

- Add lamb, reserve marinade and cook until meat is partially cooked. This takes about 2–3 minutes.

- Stir in stock and season to taste with salt and pepper. Lower heat and simmer for 10 minutes. Remove from heat.

- Ladle soup into serving bowls and serve immediately.

JAMAICAN AVOCADO SOUP

Serves 2–3

Ingredients

Avocado	1, halved, peeled and stone removed
Onion	1, peeled and grated
Lemon juice	1 Tbsp
Chicken stock	125 ml (4 fl oz / $^1/_2$ cup) (see pg 150)
Sour cream	100 ml ($3^1/_3$ fl oz)
Light (single) cream	100 ml ($3^1/_3$ fl oz)
Salt	to taste
Ground black pepper	to taste

Method

• Place avocado flesh, onion, lemon juice, stock, sour cream and 75 ml ($2^1/_2$ fl oz / 5 Tbsp) cream into a blender (processor). Purée until mixture is smooth.

• Transfer puréed mixture into a large bowl. Season with salt and pepper to taste. Transfer to refrigerator to chill until ready to serve.

• Ladle soup into serving bowls. Drizzle remaining cream into soup and serve immediately.

Note: If mixture is too thick, thin it down with milk to desired consistency.

LEMONY LAMB SOUP

Serves 4–5

Ingredients

Lamb	225 g (8 oz), thinly sliced
Garlic	2 cloves, peeled and crushed
Lamb stock	1.5 litres (48 fl oz / 6 cups) (see pg 151)
Sugar	to taste
Lemons	1/2, thinly sliced
Lemon juice	3 Tbsp
Bird's eye chillies	2, sliced (reserve some for garnish)
Light soy sauce	1 tsp
Chopped coriander (cilantro) roots	1/2 tsp
Salt	to taste
Ground black pepper	to taste

Method

- Place lamb, garlic, stock, sugar and lemon slices in a pot. Bring to the boil, then lower heat and simmer for 30 minutes, or until meat is tender.

- Stir in lemon juice, chillies, soy sauce and coriander roots. Season with salt and pepper to taste.

- Ladle soup into bowls, garnish with reserved chillies and serve with white rice.

TOMATO ORANGE SOUP

Serves 6–8

Ingredients

Butter	2 Tbsp
Minced onion	15 g ($\frac{1}{2}$ oz)
Garlic	1 clove, peeled and minced
Carrot	50 g (2 oz), peeled and minced
Celery	1 stalk, chopped
Plain (all-purpose) flour	30 g (1 oz)
Chicken stock	650 ml (21 fl oz / $2\frac{5}{8}$ cups) (see pg 150)
Orange juice	250 ml (8 fl oz / 1 cup)
Tomatoes	4, chopped
Tomato paste	15 g ($\frac{1}{2}$ oz)
Salt	to taste
Ground black pepper	to taste

Garnish

Chopped parsley leaves

Method

- Heat butter in a pot. Fry onion, garlic, carrot and celery for 3–4 minutes. Stir in flour and mix well.

- Add chicken stock, orange juice, tomatoes and tomato paste. Season with salt and pepper to taste. Simmer, uncovered, for 25 minutes.

- Pour mixture into a blender (processor) and purée until smooth. Strain soup purée and discard pulp.

- Serve either as a hot or cold soup. If serving hot, reheat before serving. If serving cold, transfer soup to refrigerator to chill until ready to serve. Ladle soup into serving bowls, garnish with parsley and serve.

APRICOT LENTIL SOUP

Serves 6–8

Ingredients

Ingredient	
Lamb stock	2 litres (64 fl oz / 8 cups) (see pg 151)
Onion	1, peeled and sliced
Red lentils	100 g (3^1/$_2$ oz)
Potatoes	50 g (1^2/$_3$ oz), peeled and diced
Dried apricots	50 g (1^2/$_3$ oz), diced
Fresh apricots	100 g (3^1/$_2$ oz), peeled, stoned and diced
Garam masala	2 tsp
Salt	to taste
Ground black pepper	to taste
Lemon juice	to taste

Method

- Place lamb stock, onion and lentils in a large saucepan. Bring mixture to the boil. Reduce heat, cover and simmer for 20 minutes, or until lentils are soft.

- Add potatoes, apricots and garam masala and cook until potatoes are soft.

- Season with salt, pepper and lemon juice to taste. Ladle into bowls and serve.

MANGO SOUP

Serves 4

Ingredients

Ripe mango	1, peeled, stone removed and cubed
Sweet potato	1, peeled and cubed
Fresh milk	100 ml (3^1/$_3$ fl oz / ^{2}/$_5$ cup)
Evaporated milk	100 ml (3^1/$_3$ fl oz / ^{2}/$_5$ cup)
Salt	to taste
Ground black pepper	^{1}/$_2$ tsp
Sugar (optional)	to taste

Method

- Steam mango and sweet potato over moderate heat for 8–10 minutes, or until sweet potato is soft.

- Purée steamed mango and sweet potato in a blender (processor) until a smooth paste is formed.

- Heat milk and evaporated milk in a saucepan over medium heat until small bubbles are visible. Gradually stir in purée. Mix well and bring mixture to the boil. Season with salt, pepper and sugar, if desired.

- Ladle into serving bowls and serve with bread.

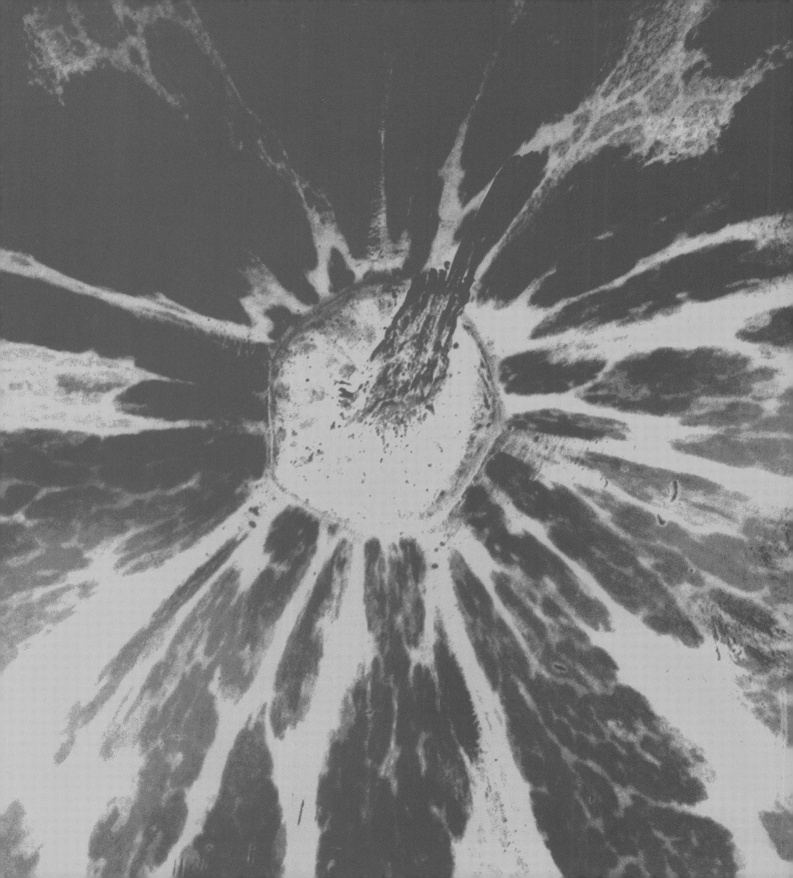

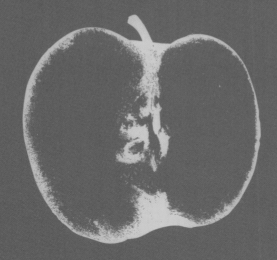

RICE

"The pleasure of the table is of all ages, conditions, countries and times."

Brillat – Savarin

FRIED RICE WITH PINEAPPLE

Serves 4

Ingredients

Pineapple	1, approximately 2 kg (4 lb 6 oz)
Cooking oil	60 ml (2 fl oz / ½ cup)
Garlic	1 clove, peeled and crushed
Onion	1 large, peeled and minced
Red chillies	3, seeded and sliced
Lean pork	125 g (4½ oz), sliced
Dried prawn (shrimp) powder (optional)	1 tsp
Eggs	2, lightly beaten
Boiled Basmati rice	400 g (14 oz)
Prawns (shrimps)	200 g (7 oz), peeled and cleaned
Spring onions (scallions)	3, chopped
Salt	to taste

Method

- Lie pineapple on its side. Slice off one-quarter lengthways and set aside to use as lid. Scoop out pineapple flesh and discard core. Cube 500 g (1 lb ½ oz) pineapple flesh and save remaining pineapple flesh for other use.

- Heat oil in a frying pan. Fry garlic, onion and chillies until light brown.

- Add pork and cook for 1 minute, stirring constantly.

- Stir in eggs and dried prawn powder, if desired.

- Add rice, prawns, pineapple and spring onions. Cook for 1 minute, stirring and tossing ingredients. Season with salt to taste.

- Spoon hot fried rice into pineapple shell and cover with lid so the rice absorbs the flavour of the pineapple. Set aside for 5 minutes before serving.

Note: Use day-old rice as it is drier than freshly cooked rice, enabling it to absorb more flavour. Alternatively, cook rice a few hours in advance and leave it out for 3–4 hours to dry before using.

TOMATO RICE

Serves 3–4

Ingredients

Butter	60 g (2 oz)
Garlic	2 cloves, peeled and minced
Onion	1, peeled and sliced
Cardamoms	2 pods, crushed
Cinnamon	1 stick, about 5 cm (2 in) long + extra for garnishing
Cloves	2
Rice	225 g (7$^1/_2$ oz)
Tomato juice	450 ml (15 fl oz / 1$^5/_8$ cups)
Milk	1 Tbsp
Salt	to taste

Method

- Heat butter in a frying pan. Fry garlic until it turns golden brown.

- Add onion, cardamoms, cinnamon and cloves. Fry until onion is soft and translucent and spices are fragrant.

- Add rice, tomato juice, milk and salt. Gently stir ingredients together.

- Cover pot and cook rice for 20–25 minutes, or until liquid has been absorbed. Remove from heat.

- Using a fork, fluff rice then replace cover and let rice cook thoroughly in its own steam for at least 5 minutes. Garnish as desired before serving.

PEACH RICE

Serves 5–6

Ingredients

Butter	60 g (2 oz)
Mustard seeds	1 tsp
Split black gram	1 tsp
Chilli powder	$\frac{1}{2}$ tsp
Grated coconut	120 g (4 oz)
Peaches	450 g (16 oz), sliced
Ground turmeric	$\frac{1}{2}$ tsp
Cashew nuts	12, chopped
Raisins	20 g ($\frac{2}{3}$ oz)
Salt	to taste
Cooked long-grain rice	1 kg (2 lb 3 oz), kept warm
Coriander leaves (cilantro)	3 sprigs, chopped

Method

- Heat butter in a frying pan and add mustard seeds, black gram and chilli powder.

- When mustard seeds begin to splutter, add coconut and peaches and fry for 5–7 minutes. Add ground turmeric, cashew nuts, raisins and salt and fry for another 2 minutes.

- Stir mixture into cooked rice and mix well. Transfer to serving bowls, mix in coriander leaves and serve on its own or with a chicken dish.

LEMON RICE

Serves 3–4

Ingredients

Rice	225 g (7½ oz)
Ground turmeric	½ tsp
Saffron threads	4
Sesame oil or coconut oil	1 Tbsp
Mustard seeds	½ tsp
Bengal gram	1 tsp
Black gram	1 tsp
Dried chilli	1, soaked to soften then cut into 3 pieces
Curry leaves	1 sprig
Lemon juice	2 Tbsp
Salt	to taste

Method

- Cook rice in a rice cooker and transfer to large bowl. While rice is still hot, add turmeric and saffron and mix well until rice is evenly coated. Set aside and allow to cool.

- Heat oil in frying pan. Add mustard seeds, bengal and black gram, chilli and curry leaves. When mustard seeds splutter, remove from heat and pour mixture over rice.

- Add lemon juice to rice and mix well. Season to taste with salt. Transfer rice to serving bowls and serve either hot or cold.

COCONUT RICE WITH GREEN BEANS

Serves 3–4

Ingredients

Long-grained rice	225 g (7$\frac{1}{2}$ oz), washed
Green (mung) beans	50 g (2 oz), washed
Coconut milk	500 ml (16 fl oz / 2 cups)
Screwpine (*pandan*) leaf	1
Cinnamon	1 stick, about 5 cm (2 in) length
Cardamoms	2 pods, crushed
Salt	a pinch

Method

- Combine all ingredients in a medium saucepan. Bring to the boil, stirring, then leave to cook over low heat until coconut milk is completely absorbed.

- Discard cinnamon stick and screwpine leaf.

- Cover and cook over low heat for a further 10 minutes. Serve hot with a prawn dish.

STEAMED RICE AND BANANA

Makes 24 parcels

Ingredients

Glutinous rice	450 g (1 lb), soaked for 3–4 hours and drained
Coconut milk	500 ml (16 fl oz / 2 cups)
Sugar	250 g (9 oz)
Salt	1/2 tsp
Banana leaves	24 sheets, each 15 x 15-cm (6 x 6-in)
Bananas	6, peeled, sliced lengthways and halved
Coconut cream	100 ml (3^1/$_3$ fl oz / 5/8 cup)

Method

- Combine rice and coconut milk in a pot. Cook, stirring occasionally, until rice is almost cooked and moist.

- Stir in sugar and salt and mix well. Remove from heat and transfer to a large bowl. Set aside to cool.

- Spoon 3 Tbsp rice mixture onto the centre of each banana leaf. Place a banana slice on top of rice mixture.

- Fold 2 opposite sides of leaf over filling, then tuck open ends under. Repeat to make 24 parcels.

- Arrange banana leaf parcels in a steamer. Steam for 30–40 minutes, or until rice is cooked. Allow guest to unwrap the parcels themselves. Drizzle some coconut cream before eating.

Note: When steamed, banana leaves provide additional flavour and aroma to the rice. However, aluminium foil can be used as an alternative if banana leaves are unavailable.

ORANGE RICE

Serves 2–3

Butter	20 g ($^3/_4$ oz)
Long-grained rice	225 g ($7^1/_2$ oz)
Orange juice	450 ml (15 fl oz / $1^4/_5$ cup)
Salt	a pinch
Parsley leaves	1 sprig

Method

- Heat butter in a frying pan. Add rice and fry until translucent.

- Add orange juice and salt. Cook mixture over moderate heat for 20–25 minutes, or until orange juice is absorbed and rice is light and fluffy.

- Transfer rice to a serving dish. Garnish with parsley and serve hot with a poultry dish.

STRAWBERRY RICE

Serves 3–4

Ingredients

Coconut milk	100 ml (3$^1/_2$ fl oz / $^5/_8$ cup)
Cardamoms	2 pods, crushed
Castor (superfine) sugar	100 g (3$^1/_2$ oz)
Strawberries	6, hulled and cubed
Honey (optional)	1 Tbsp
Butter	1 Tbsp
Raisins	1 Tbsp
Chopped cashew nuts	1 Tbsp
Cooked Basmati rice	225 g (8 oz)
Salt	to taste

Method

- Heat coconut milk and cardamoms in a saucepan until mixture comes to the boil. Stir in sugar, strawberries and honey, if desired.

- Cover pan and simmer mixture until coconut milk is thickened. Remove from heat and set aside.

- Heat butter in a frying pan. Fry raisins and cashew nuts until cashews brown.

- In a large mixing bowl, combine rice, raisins, cashews and coconut milk mixture. Season with salt and mix well. Serve hot on its own.

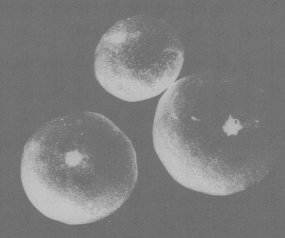

MEAT AND POULTRY

"I want there to be no peasant in my realm so poor that he will not have a chicken in his pot every Sunday."

Henry IV, France

SPICY APPLE-PEACH TOPPED PORK CHOPS

Serves 4

Ingredients

Pork chops	4, about 200 g (7 oz) each
Canned peaches	425 g (15 oz), drained, sliced and reserve syrup
Apples	2, peeled, thinly sliced
Brown sugar	4 tsp
Corn flour (cornstarch)	2 tsp
Coconut milk	60 ml (2 fl oz / $^1/_4$ cup)

Marinade

Cooking oil	2 Tbsp
Lemon juice	60 ml (2 fl oz / $^1/_4$ cup)
Chilli powder	$^1/_2$ tsp
Garam masala	$^1/_4$ tsp
Salt	to taste
Ground black pepper	to taste

Method

- Prepare marinade. Combine all marinade ingredients with a whisk. Mix well and set aside.

- Arrange pork chops in a flat dish and spoon over marinade. Leave pork chops to marinate for 30 minutes, turning over once. Reserve marinade.

- Oil and heat grill. Brush pork chops with marinade and grill for 5 minutes. Turn chops over and brush with marinade. Grill for another 5–7 minutes, depending on thickness of chops.

- Divide peaches into 4 portions. Place one portion on each pork chop. Top with apples and sprinkle 1 tsp sugar over apples. Grill for another 3 minutes or until fruit is heated through and sugar starts to caramelise. This will take 3–5 minutes. Transfer to serving dish.

- In a small saucepan, mix corn flour with coconut milk until it forms a smooth paste. Add reserved peach syrup and stir in remaining marinade.

- Bring mixture to the boil. Stir constantly and for cook 1 minute.

- Drizzle sauce over pork chops and serve remaining sauce in sauce bowl. Serve hot with mashed potatoes and a salad of your choice.

PINEAPPLE AND CHICKEN CURRY

Serves 4–5

Ingredients

Chicken drumsticks	5, each about 110 g (4 oz)
Salt	to taste
Cooking oil for deep-frying	
Pineapple	1/2, small, peeled, cored and cut into wedges
Tomato ketchup	100 ml (3 1/2 fl oz / 2/5 cup)
Chilli sauce	100 ml (3 1/2 fl oz / 2/5 cup)
Warm water	250 ml (8 fl oz / 1 cup)

Curry Paste

Shallots	10, peeled and roughly chopped
Ginger	5-cm (2-in) knob, peeled and roughly chopped
Garlic	2 cloves, peeled and roughly chopped
Red chillies	15, each cut into 3 pieces
Dried chillies	5, soaked to soften, then roughly cut
Dried prawns (shrimps)	30 g (1 oz), toasted
Salt	to taste

Method

- Prepare curry paste. Combine all curry paste ingredients in a blender (processor) until finely ground. Set aside.

- Season chicken with 1 tsp salt and set aside to marinate for 15 minutes.

- Heat oil for deep-frying and gently lower in chicken drumsticks. Deep-fry until golden brown. Drain well and set aside. Reserve 1 Tbsp warm oil.

- Heat a saucepan and add warm oil. Fry curry paste until fragrant. Add chicken and pineapple wedges. Cook for 5 minutes ensuring chicken is well-coated with curry paste.

- Add tomato ketchup, chilli sauce and water. Stir to mix and bring to the boil. Reduce heat and simmer for 10–15 minutes.

- Check seasoning and adjust to taste with salt. Transfer to a serving bowl and serve with rice.

BANANA AND LAMB CURRY

Serves 4

Ingredients

Butter	$^1/_2$ Tbsp
Bay leaf	1
Onion	1, peeled and sliced
Garlic	3 cloves, peeled and minced
Ground fennel	1 tsp
Chilli powder	2 tsp
Ground coriander	2 tsp
Ground turmeric	$^1/_2$ tsp
Salt	to taste
Lamb chops	4, about 225 g (7$^1/_2$ oz) each
Water	60 ml (2 fl oz / $^1/_4$ cup)
Coconut cream	150 ml (5 fl oz / $^5/_8$ cup)
Bananas	2, peeled and sliced

Method

• Heat butter in frying pan. Fry bay leaf, onion, garlic and ground fennel until fragrant.

• Add chilli powder, coriander, turmeric and salt and fry for 1 minute. Add lamb chops and water. Bring to the boil, reduce heat and simmer for 10–15 minutes, or until lamb is nearly cooked.

• Stir in coconut cream and bananas. Simmer until gravy thickens. Transfer to a serving dish and serve hot with rice.

CURRIED TOMATO AND BEEF

Serves 4–6

Ingredients

Cooking oil	60 ml (2 fl oz / ¼ cup)
Shallots	15, peeled and finely sliced
Garlic	5 cloves, peeled and finely sliced
Ginger	5-cm (2-in) knob, peeled and grated
Curry leaves	a handful
Chilli powder	1 tsp
Ground fennel	2 tsp
Ground cumin	1 tsp
Beef	450 g (1 lb), cut into 2.5-cm (1-in) cubes
Water	250 ml (8 fl oz / 1 cup)
Salt	to taste
Sugar	to taste
Tomato purée	1 can
Coconut cream	60 ml (2 fl oz / ¼ cup)

Method

- Heat oil in a saucepan. Fry shallots, garlic, ginger and curry leaves until fragrant.

- Add chilli powder, fennel and cumin and fry until fragrant.

- Add meat and fry for a few minutes until meat browns.

- Add water, salt and sugar. Bring to the boil, then reduce heat and simmer until meat is tender.

- Stir in tomato purée and coconut cream and mix well. Transfer to a serving bowl and serve immediately with hot rice.

MINCED PORK AND ORANGE SEGMENTS

Serves 5–6

Ingredients

Cooking oil	2 Tbsp
Garlic	3 cloves, peeled and minced
Shallots	2, peeled and finely chopped
Minced pork	125 g (4^1/$_2$ oz)
Light soy sauce	1 Tbsp
Brown sugar	1 Tbsp
Ground black pepper	to taste
Salt	to taste
Chopped roasted peanuts	3 Tbsp
Canned mandarin oranges	330 g (11 oz)

Garnish

Lettuce	3–4 leaves
Red chillies	3, seeded and cut into thin strips
Coriander leaves (cilantro)	1 sprig, sliced

Method

- Heat oil in a frying pan. Add garlic and shallots and fry until garlic turns light brown.

- Add pork, soy sauce, sugar, pepper and salt. Fry until pork is pale in colour and cooked.

- Stir in peanuts and mix well. Remove from heat and mix in mandarin oranges.

- To serve, arrange lettuce leaves in a bowl. Spoon pork and orange mixture onto leaves. Garnish with chillies and coriander and serve.

FILLET OF PORK WITH PRUNES

Serves 6–8

Ingredients

Pork fillet	1 kg (2 lb 3 oz)
Prunes	500 g (1 lb 1½ oz), stoned and syrup
Salt	to taste
Ground black pepper	to taste
Bacon	4 slices
Ground cinnamon	¼ Tbsp
Coriander leaves (cilantro)	1 sprig, chopped

Method

• Preheat oven to 180°C (350°F).

• Using a sharp knife, slice pork fillet almost half in length. Open out and place prunes down the middle. Fold fillet to enclose prunes.

• Season fillet with salt and pepper. Wrap bacon around pork fillet.

• Place meat in a shallow casserole. Bake in oven for 50 minutes.

• Add prune syrup, cinnamon and coriander leaves to casserole and continue to bake for a further 15 minutes, basting frequently. Remove from oven and let meat rest for 5 minutes. Transfer to a serving dish and serve with bread or rice.

RUSSIAN BEEF STROGANOFF

Serves 4–6

Ingredients

Beef	1 kg (2 lb 3 oz), thinly sliced
Salt	to taste
Ground black pepper	to taste
Butter	70 g (2^1/$_2$ oz)
Green chillies	2, minced
Tomatoes	3, cut into wedges or 2^1/$_2$ Tbsp tomato purée
Sour cream	100 ml (3^1/$_2$ fl oz / ^{2}/$_5$ cup)
Onion	^{1}/$_4$, peeled and grated

Method

- Season beef with salt and pepper and set aside for 10 minutes.

- Heat butter in a frying pan. Add chillies and beef and fry until beef browns.

- Stir in tomatoes and sour cream. Simmer mixture over low heat for 10–15 minutes. Adjust seasoning to taste.

- Stir in onion and transfer to a serving dish. Serve immediately with white rice or bread.

SWEET AND SOUR PORK

Serves 4–5

Ingredients

Egg	1, beaten
Plain (all-purpose) flour	3 Tbsp
Salt	to taste
Ground black pepper	to taste
Pork	300 g (10$\frac{1}{2}$ oz), cut into 3-cm (1$\frac{1}{2}$-in) cubes
Cooking oil for deep-frying	

Sweet and Sour Sauce

Cooking oil	2 Tbsp
Red chillies	2, sliced
Green capsicum (bell pepper)	1, seeded and chopped
Canned pineapple cubes	225 g (8$\frac{1}{2}$ oz), drained and reserve syrup
Corn flour (cornstarch)	1 Tbsp, mixed with 2 Tbsp water
Salt	a pinch
Cider vinegar	2 Tbsp
Light soy sauce	$\frac{1}{2}$ Tbsp

Method

- Combine egg and flour in a mixing bowl to form a batter. Season with salt and pepper. Coat pork with batter evenly.

- Heat oil for deep-frying. Gently lower coated pork pieces and deep-fry until lightly browned. Drain well and set aside.

- Prepare sauce. Heat oil in a saucepan. Fry chillies and capsicum for 3 minutes. Add pineapple, syrup and corn flour mixture and stir until mixture is smooth. Add salt and cider vinegar. Bring to the boil and simmer for 3–5 minutes before removing from heat.

- Add fried pork pieces into sauce. Toss and coat evenly. Transfer to a serving dish and serve hot.

SEAFOOD

"Let no man fancy he knows how to dine
Till he has learnt how to taste and taste combine".

Horace

TOMATO AND FISH CURRY

Serves 6–8

Ingredients

Onions	2, large, peeled and sliced
Garlic	3 cloves, peeled
Mustard oil	30 ml (1 fl oz)
Curry leaves	a handful
Tomatoes	200 g (7 oz), blanched and sliced
Yoghurt	200 ml (6^1/$_2$ fl oz / ^{4}/$_5$ cup)
Ground turmeric	^{1}/$_2$ tsp
Ground cumin	1 tsp
Garam masala	1 tsp
Ground cardamom	^{1}/$_4$ tsp
Mustard seeds	^{1}/$_4$ tsp
Salt	to taste
White fish steaks (cod or grouper)	6, each about 2-cm (1-in) thick, clean and pat dry

Method

• Combine onions and garlic in a blender (processor) to form a smooth paste.

• Heat oil in a deep saucepan. Fry paste until oil separates from paste. Add all remaining ingredients except fish and cook for 15 minutes.

• Add fish, cover pot and simmer for 5 minutes or until fish is cooked. Transfer to a serving dish and serve immediately with rice or bread.

CURRIED APPLE AND PRAWNS WITH PINEAPPLE JUICE

Serves 6–8

Ingredients

Margarine	60 g (2 oz)
Curry powder	1 Tbsp
Chilli powder	1/4 tsp
Minced onion	1 Tbsp
Garlic	2 cloves, peeled and crushed
Red chillies	2, seeded and sliced
Prawns (shrimps)	1 kg (2 lb 3 oz), shelled with tails intact and deveined
Apples	2, peeled and sliced
Unsweetened pineapple juice	250 ml (8 fl oz / 1 cup)
Coconut cream	150 ml (5 fl oz / 5/8 cup)

Method

- Melt margarine in a saucepan. Add curry and chilli powders and fry for 2 minutes.

- Add onion, garlic, chillies and prawns. Stir-fry over high heat until onion is soft.

- Stir in apples, then add pineapple juice and coconut cream. Bring mixture to the boil and continue stirring until mixture thickens. Transfer to a serving dish and serve immediately.

PINEAPPLE CRAB DELIGHT

Serves 4–5

Ingredients

Butter	60 g (2 oz)
Crabs	4, cleaned and quartered
Pineapple	1, small, skinned, cut into wedges
Coconut milk	300 ml (10 fl oz / 1¼ cups)
Salt	to taste
Coconut cream	150 ml (5 fl oz / ⅝ cup)

Seasoning

Dried chillies	15, soaked to soften then roughly cut
Shallots	15, peeled and roughly chopped
Lemon grass	1 stalk, cut into short lengths
Garlic	2 cloves, peeled
Coriander seeds	15 g (½ oz)
Curry powder	2 Tbsp
Salt	to taste

Method

- Prepare seasoning. Combine all seasoning ingredients in a blender (processor) until ingredients are finely ground.

- Heat butter in a wok. Sauté seasoning ingredients until fragrant.

- Add crabs and stir until mixture is well mixed. Cook for 5 minutes.

- Add pineapple, coconut milk and salt to taste. Simmer for 10–15 minutes.

- Add coconut cream and allow mixture to return to the boil. When mixture comes to the boil, remove from heat. Transfer to a serving dish and serve immediately.

PEACH AND PRAWN CURRY

Serves 6–8

Ingredients

Butter	1 Tbsp
Onion	1, small, peeled and minced
Garlic	3 cloves, peeled
Cinnamon	1 stick, about 5-cm (2-in) length
Cardamom	3 pods, bruised
Ground coriander	1 tsp
Chilli powder	1 tsp
Ground cumin	1½ tsp
Salt	to taste
Peaches	2 large, medium-ripe, stoned and sliced
King prawns (shrimps)	5, shelled and deveined
Coconut milk	250 ml (8 fl oz / 1 cup)
Sugar	1 tsp

Method

- Heat butter in a saucepan. Fry onion, garlic, cinnamon and cardamom over medium heat, stirring frequently until onion is soft and translucent.

- Add coriander, chilli, cumin and salt and fry for 1 minute.

- Add peaches and prawns. Stir and coat evenly with spice mixture.

- Pour in coconut milk and sugar. Bring mixture to simmering point, stirring constantly. Leave pan uncovered and simmer for another 3–4 minutes, or until peaches are tender but not mushy. Serve immediately.

SPANISH MACKEREL

Serves 4–5

Ingredients

Butter	60 g (2 oz)
Celery	90 g (3 oz), shredded
Onion	1, large, peeled and chopped
Apples	2, peeled and diced
Mackerel steaks	4, each about 2-cm (1-in) thick, cleaned and pat dry
Salt	to taste
Ground black pepper	to taste
Tomato purée	40 ml (1¹/₃ fl oz)
Coconut milk	100 ml (3¹/₃ fl oz / ²/₅ cup)

Method

- Preheat oven to 225°C (450°F).

- Heat butter in a small ovenproof dish. Add celery, onion and apples and sauté for 3 minutes. Remove from heat.

- Place fish over vegetables. Season with salt and pepper.

- Combine tomato purée with coconut milk in a small bowl. Mix well and pour over fish.

- Transfer dish to oven and bake uncovered for 10–15 minutes, or until fish is cooked. Transfer to a serving dish and serve immediately.

CITRUS FISH

Serves 6–8

Ingredients

White fish steaks	6, each about 2-cm (1-in) thick, cleaned and pat dry
Salt	to taste
Ground black pepper	to taste
Orange	1, squeezed for juice
Lemon	1, squeezed for juice
Water	

Method

• Preheat oven to 180°C (350°F).

• Arrange fish steaks in a greased baking dish. Ensure fish steaks do not overlap.

• Season fish steaks with salt and pepper. Pour in orange juice, lemon juice and just enough water to cover fish.

• Transfer to oven and bake for 10–15 minutes, or until fish is cooked. Garnish as desired and serve immediately.

FIERY PRAWNS WITH GREEN GRAPES

Serves 6–8

Ingredients

Cooking oil	75 ml (2$\frac{1}{2}$ fl oz / $\frac{1}{3}$ cup)
Large prawns (shrimps)	700 g (1$\frac{1}{2}$ lb), deveined retaining shell
Garlic	3 cloves, peeled and crushed
Ginger	1-cm ($\frac{1}{2}$-in) knob, peeled and minced
Curry leaves	1 sprig
Green grapes	100 g (3$\frac{1}{2}$ oz)
White wine	2 tsp

Seasoning

Tomato sauce	2 Tbsp
Chilli sauce	1 Tbsp
Sugar	1 tsp
Water	60 ml (2 fl oz / $\frac{1}{4}$ cup)
Salt	a pinch

Method

- Prepare seasoning. Combine all seasoning ingredients in a bowl. Mix well and set aside.

- Heat 60 ml (2 fl oz / $\frac{1}{4}$ cup) oil in a clean wok. Stir-fry prawns until the colour changes. Transfer prawns to a plate and set aside.

- Heat remaining oil in the same wok. Sauté garlic, ginger and curry leaves until fragrant. Add grapes and seasoning mixture. Simmer for 1–2 minutes.

- Return prawns to the wok. Toss and mix well. Add wine and cook for 2 minutes, allowing alcohol to evaporate. Transfer to a serving dish and serve immediately with white rice.

VEGETABLES, SALADS & PICKLES

"Accompaniments or side dishes, like the tributaries of the river, feed the main stream. They add zest to any meal."

Hindu saying

TOMATO AND CAPSICUM SALAD

Serves 8–10

Ingredients

Red capsicum (bell pepper)	1, seeded and diced
Cooking oil	30 ml (1 fl oz)
Onions	2, small, peeled and minced
Garlic	3 cloves, peeled and chopped
Green chillies	2, seeded and minced
Ripe tomatoes	600 g (1 lb 5 oz), skinned and chopped
White wine	125 ml (4 fl oz / 1/2 cup)
Chopped fresh basil	1 tsp
Salt	to taste
Ground black pepper	to taste

Method

- Bring a small pot of salted water to the boil. Reduce heat, add capsicum and simmer for 3 minutes. Drain well and set aside.

- Heat oil in a frying pan. Sauté onions, garlic and chillies until onions turn translucent. Gradually add capsicum and stir-fry for another 1–2 minutes.

- Add tomatoes, wine, basil, salt and pepper. Simmer over low heat for 20 minutes, then transfer to a serving dish. Serve warm with rice.

ORANGE-FLAVOURED CARROT

Serves 6–8

Ingredients

Butter	2 Tbsp
Orange juice	250 ml (8 fl oz / 1 cup)
Sugar	50 g (2 oz)
Baby carrots	450 g (16 oz), peeled and diced
Grated nutmeg	a pinch
Ground cardamom	a pinch

Method

- Melt butter in a pan over low heat.

- Add orange juice and sugar. Stir for 3 minutes to dissolve sugar.

- Add carrots, nutmeg and cardamom. Cook, stirring occasionally until almost all liquid has evaporated. Remove from heat.

- Serve either hot or cold. Serve immediately if serving hot or chill in the refrigerator for at least 1 hour if serving cold. Serve with poultry or meat dishes.

TOMATO CREOLE

Serves 6–8

Ingredients

Butter	60 g (2 oz)
Red chilli	1, seeded and chopped
Onion	1, large, peeled and minced
Garlic	1 clove, peeled and crushed
Yellow capsicums (bell peppers)	2, seeded and chopped
Brussels sprouts	250 g (9 oz), or 1 head cabbage, trimmed and cut across the base
Tomatoes	450 g (16 oz), skinned and cut into wedges

Seasoning

Dried basil	$1/4$ tsp
Ground black pepper	$1/4$ tsp
Salt	to taste

Method

- Melt butter in a frying pan. Add chilli, onion, garlic and capsicums and stir-fry for 5–7 minutes.

- Add brussesl sprouts or cabbage, tomatoes and seasoning. Reduce heat, cover and cook until brussels sprouts or cabbage leaves are tender. Serve hot.

BAKED SWEET POTATOES AND DATES

Serves 4–5

Ingredients

Sweet potatoes	2, large
Butter	50 g (2 oz) + 30 g (1 oz) melted
Orange juice	40 ml (1¼ fl oz)
Brown sugar	30 g (1 oz)
Grated nutmeg	a pinch
Salt	a pinch
Dried dates	8, soaked to soften and chopped

Method

- Preheat oven to 180°C (350°F).

- Place sweet potatoes in a pot and cover with cold water. Bring to the boil and cook until sweet potatoes are soft. Drain sweet potatoes, then peel and mash.

- Combine mashed sweet potatoes with melted butter, orange juice, brown sugar, nutmeg and salt. Mix evenly.

- Stir in chopped dates.

- Spoon mixture into a greased shallow casserole. Dot with a little butter and bake uncovered for 25 minutes. Scoop mixture into serving bowls and serve immediately.

APPLE PICKLE

Makes 3 cups

Ingredients

Red chillies	75 g (2¹/₂ oz)
Garlic	50 g (2 oz)
White vinegar	250 ml (8 fl oz / 1 cup)
Brown sugar	500 g (1 lb 1¹/₂ oz)
Green apples	1 kg (2 lb 3 oz) peeled, cored and chopped
Raisins	125 g (4¹/₂ oz)
Ginger	2.5-cm (1-in) knob, peeled and minced
Salt	to taste

Method

- Combine chillies and garlic in a blender (processor) until fine.

- Place vinegar and sugar in a saucepan over low heat. Bring to the boil stirring constantly until sugar dissolves.

- Add apples and raisins. Gently cook until apples are tender.

- Add remaining ingredients and continue to cook till pickle is thick or of the consistency of jam. Season to taste with salt. Remove from heat and set aside to cool.

- Store in an airtight jar for up to 3 months at room temperature.

Note: Always use clean utensils to dish out pickles. This will prevent contamination of the contents of the jar.

MIXED PICKLE

Makes 2 cups

Ingredients

Green mangoes	500 g (1 lb 1^1/$_2$ oz), peeled, stoned and cut into bite-size pieces
Limes	6, cut into quarters
Carrots	50 g (2 oz), peeled and cut into bite-size pieces
Turnip	50 g (2 oz), peeled and cut into bite-size pieces
Salt	100 g (4 oz)
Mustard oil	250 ml (8 fl oz / 1 cup)
Green chillies	50 g (2 oz)
Ground turmeric	30 g (1 oz)
Ground coriander	20 g (^{2}/$_3$ oz)
Chilli powder	125 g (4^1/$_2$ oz)

Method

- Combine mangoes, limes, carrots and turnip with salt in a large mixing bowl and mix well. Transfer mixture onto a tray and spread out evenly. Sun-dry mixture for 12 hours.

- Heat oil in a frying pan. Add chillies, turmeric, coriander and chilli powder. Heat through, then remove from heat. Set aside to cool.

- Combine sun-dried mixture and flavoured oil in a jar. Set aside to pickle for 10 days, shaking the jar every day.

- Store in an airtight jar for up to 3 months at room temperature.

AVOCADO SALAD

Serves 2

Ingredients

Avocado	2, peeled, stoned and cut into small cubes
Cooked turkey breast	100 g (3^1/$_2$ oz), thinly sliced
Mango	100 g (3^1/$_2$ oz), peeled, stoned and cut into cubes

Salad Dressing

Olive oil	1 tsp
Lemon juice	2 tsp
Mustard powder	a pinch
Ground white pepper	a pinch
Salt	to taste

Method

- Prepare salad dressing. Whisk together olive oil, lemon juice and mustard powder in a small bowl. Season with pepper and salt to taste, then set aside.

- Combine avocado, turkey breast and mango together in a salad bowl. Drizzle salad dressing over, toss well and serve.

BANANAS IN SPICED YOGHURT

Serves 4–5

Ingredients

Yoghurt	250 ml (8 fl oz / 1 cup)
Lemon juice	30 ml (1 fl oz)
Grated coconut	30 g (1 oz)
Crushed rock sugar	30 g (1 oz)
Salt	$^1/_2$ tsp
Chilli powder	$^1/_4$ tsp
Bananas	2, peeled and sliced
Butter	1 tsp
Cumin seeds	$^1/_2$ tsp
Mustard seeds	$^1/_2$ tsp

Method

- Combine yoghurt, lemon juice, grated coconut, rock sugar, salt, chilli powder and bananas in a bowl.

- Heat butter in a frying pan. Fry cumin seeds and mustard seeds until mustard seeds splutter, then remove from heat.

- Pour spiced mixture over banana mixture and mix well.

- Serve as an accompaniment to a rice meal.

CREAM CHEESE FRUIT SALAD

Serves 4–5

Ingredients

Canned mandarin oranges	200 g (7 oz), drained
Grapes	400 g (14 oz), halved and seeded
Red apple	1, large, cored and diced
Pears	150 g (5 oz), cored and sliced
Almond slivers	150 g (5 oz)
Lettuce leaves	4

Cream Cheese Dressing

Cream cheese	100 g ($3^1/_2$ oz), softened
Honey	30 ml (1 fl oz)
Lemon juice	60 ml (2 fl oz / $^1/_4$ cup)
Orange juice	80 ml ($2^1/_2$ fl oz / $^1/_3$ cup)
Salt	to taste

Method

- Prepare cream cheese dressing. Whisk together all the dressing ingredients and beat until smooth. Transfer to the refrigerator to chill.

- Combine oranges, grapes, apple, pears and almonds, mix well.

- Toss fruit mixture with cream cheese dressing. Mix evenly.

- Arrange lettuce leaves on a serving dish. Spoon fruit mixture over lettuce leaves and serve.

MOLASSES FRUIT SALAD

Serves 3–4

Ingredients

Canned pineapple	200 g (7 oz), diced
Oranges	4, peeled and cut into bite-size pieces
Onion	1, peeled and sliced
Boiled beetroot	1, sliced
Pear	1, peeled, cored and cubed
Grapefruits	2, peeled and segmented
Lettuce leaves	4

Dressing

Olive oil	180 ml (6 fl oz / $^3/_4$ cup)
Lemon juice	125 ml (4 fl oz / $^1/_2$ cup)
Molasses	60 g (2 oz)
Mustard powder	1 tsp
Ground black pepper	$^1/_2$ tsp
Salt	to taste

Method

- Prepare dressing. Combine all ingredients in a screw-top jar. Replace lid firmly, shake well to mix and set aside.

- Combine pineapple, oranges, onion, beetroot, pear and grapefruit in a mixing bowl.

- Arrange lettuce leaves on a serving plate. Spoon on fruit mixture. Drizzle dressing over salad and serve.

FRUIT AND PORK SALAD

Serves 4–5

Ingredients

Apple	1, peeled and cut into cubes
Green mango	1, peeled, stoned and thinly sliced
Pineapple	200 g (7 oz), peeled and cut into cubes
Cooked pork fillet	100 g (3 1/2 oz), thinly sliced
Red capsicum (bell pepper)	1, seeded and chopped

Salad Dressing

Lemon juice	2 Tbsp
Palm sugar	1 Tbsp
Thai fish sauce	1/2 Tbsp
Chopped coriander leaves (cilantro)	1 Tbsp

Method

- Prepare salad dressing. Combine all ingredients, mix well and set aside.

- In a separate bowl, combine apple, mango, pineapple, pork and capsicum. Transfer to a serving dish. Pour dressing over salad, toss and serve.

SNACKS AND DESSERTS

"Life is uncertain. Eat dessert first."

Ernestine Ulmer

BANANA CAKE

Makes one 20-cm (8-in) square cake

Ingredients

Plain (all-purpose) flour	225 g (8 oz)
Baking powder	1 tsp
Bicarbonate of soda	1 tsp
Butter	160 g (5^1/$_2$ oz)
Sugar	160 g (5^1/$_2$ oz)
Eggs	3
Lime	1, squeezed for juice
Milk	3 Tbsp
Ground cinnamon	a pinch
Bananas	2, large, peeled and mashed

Method

- Preheat oven at 200°C (400°F).

- Sift flour, baking powder and bicarbonate of soda into a mixing bowl and set aside.

- In a clean mixing bowl, cream butter and sugar until butter is pale in colour. Beat in eggs, then add lime juice, milk and ground cinnamon.

- Add in mashed bananas in 2 parts and mix well.

- Gently fold in sifted flour mixture by hand. Mix well until a smooth batter is formed. Pour batter into a greased 20 x 20-cm (8 x 8-in) square baking tin. Bake for 40–50 minutes.

- Remove and set aside for 10 minutes to cool before removing from tin. Slice and serve with ice cream if desired.

ORANGE CUPCAKES

Makes 12 cupcakes

Ingredients

Butter	90 g (3 oz)
Sugar	90 g (3 oz)
Eggs	2
Orange	1, grated for zest and squeezed for 2 tsp juice
Plain (all-purpose) flour	120 g (4 oz), sifted
Baking powder	2 Tbsp

Method

- Preheat oven to 180°C (350°F). Line a 12-hole patty tin with paper cases or grease tins.

- Cream butter and sugar until butter is pale in colour. Gradually beat in one egg at a time, ensuring that batter is well mixed.

- Mix in zest, juice and 60 g (2 oz) flour.

- Gently fold in remaining flour and baking powder. Mix well until batter is smooth.

- Half-fill paper cases or greased patty tins with batter. Bake for 15–20 minutes, or until a toothpick comes out clean.

- Remove from oven and place cupcakes on a cooling rack. Garnish as desired and serve.

PLUM NECTARINE CHARLOTTE

Serves 4

Ingredients

Wholemeal bread	8 slices
Melted butter	150 ml (5 fl oz)
Red plums	500 g (1 lb 1¹/₂ oz), halved and stoned
Red nectarines	500 g (1 lb 1¹/₂ oz), halved and stoned
Sugar	60 g (2 oz)

Method

- Preheat oven to 200°C (400°F). Grease a 20 x 10-cm (8 x 4-in) baking dish.

- Cut bread slices to fit sides and bottom of baking dish. Chop remaining bread into coarse breadcrumbs and set aside.

- Dip cut bread slices into melted butter, then use to line the bottom and the sides of greased baking dish.

- Arrange plums and nectarines in the baking dish on top of bread layer.

- Combine breadcrumbs with remaining butter and sugar in a mixing bowl, toss and mix well. Spread breadcrumb mixture on top of fruit layer in the baking dish.

- Cover with a sheet of buttered greaseproof paper and bake for 30–40 minutes. Remove paper and continue baking until top layer of charlotte is crisp and golden. Serve warm or cold with cream.

APPLE CRUMBLE

Serves 6–8

Ingredients

Green apples	450 g (16 oz), peeled, cored and quartered
Lemon	1, grated for zest
Castor (superfine) sugar	180 g (6^1/$_2$ oz)

Crumble

Plain (all-purpose) flour	225 g (8^1/$_2$ oz)
Margarine	100 g (3^1/$_2$ oz), cut into cubes and chilled
Butter	20 g (^{2}/$_3$ oz), chilled
Demerara sugar	120 g (4 oz)
Ground cinnamon	a pinch

Method

- Preheat oven to 190°C (375°F).

- Combine apples, lemon zest and sugar in a mixing bowl, mix well and set aside.

- Prepare crumble. Sift flour into a mixing bowl. Use fingers to rub in margarine and butter until mixture resembles fine breadcrumbs. Add in sugar and cinnamon, mix well. Divide crumble mixture into 2 portions.

- Spread 1 portion of crumble mixture on the base and sides of a round 22.5-cm (9-in) diameter baking dish. Press in crumble mixture until it forms a firm crust.

- Spoon in apple mixture and spread evenly. Sprinkle in remaining crumble mixture, pressing down lightly. Bake for 1 hour, or until top of crumble is golden brown.

- Remove and allow to cool slightly. Serve either cold or hot with custard or light cream.

ORANGE SOUFFLÉ

Ingredients

Corn flour (cornstarch)	4 Tbsp
Orange juice	280 ml (9 fl oz / 1^1/$_8$ cups)
Butter	35 g (1^1/$_4$ oz)
Castor (superfine) sugar	100 g (3^1/$_2$ oz)
Large eggs	5, yolks and whites separated and beaten

Serves 4

Method

- Preheat oven to 190°C (370°F).

- Combine corn flour with 60 ml (2 fl oz / ^{1}/$_4$ cup) orange juice to form a smooth paste.

- Heat remaining juice in a saucepan with butter and sugar. Add corn flour paste and bring the mixture to the boil for 1 minute, stirring constantly.

- Remove from heat and stir in beaten egg yolks. Set aside to cool.

- Whisk egg whites until firm peaks form. Carefully fold egg whites into orange mixture.

- Pour mixture into four 10 x 5-cm (4 x 2-in) ramekins.

- Place ramekins on a baking tray and bake for 20 minutes, or until tops are brown and well risen. Remove from oven and serve immediately.

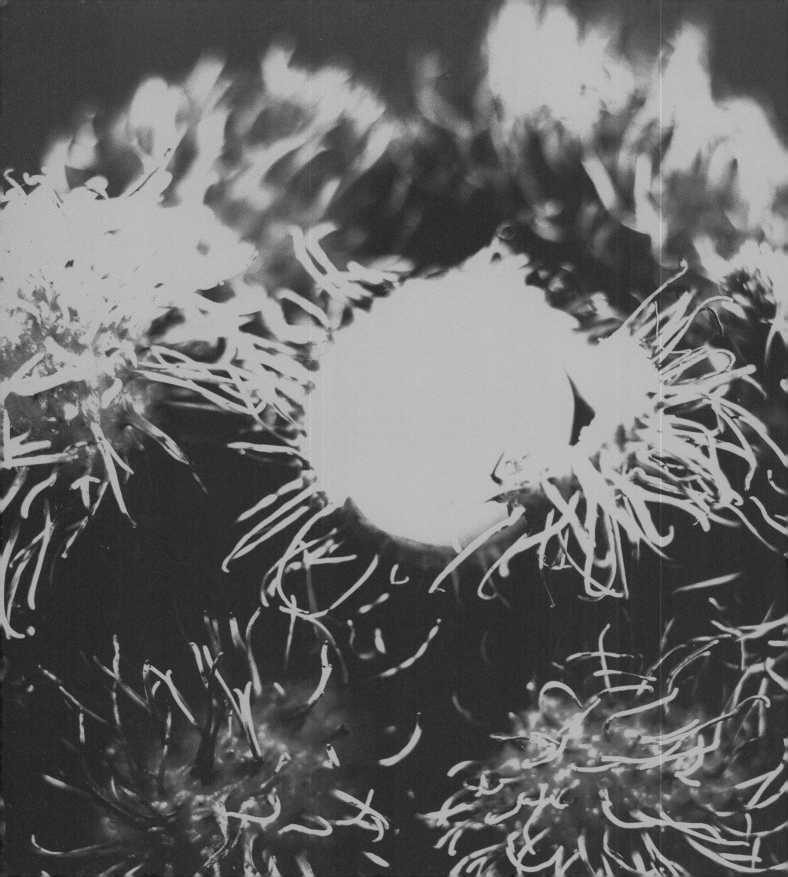

DRINKS AND ICES

"We eat food for its texture, as well as for fragrance, flavour and colour."

Asian Wisdom

PEACH SHAKE

Serves 2–3

Ingredients

Canned peaches	250 g (9 oz), chopped
Oranges	2, squeezed for juice
Sugar	to taste
Water	30 ml (1 fl oz)
Cold milk	125 ml (4 fl oz / 1/2 cup)

Garnish

Cold milk (optional)

Method

- Combine all ingredients except milk in a blender (processor) until smooth.

- Stir in milk and mix well. Strain mixture and discard pulp.

- Refrigerate until ready to serve. Pour into glasses and swirl in some cold milk for garnish, if desired before serving.

PASSION FRUIT PUNCH

Makes about 1.25 litres (40 fl oz / 5 cups)

Ingredients

Black tea	1 litre (32 fl oz / 4 cups), chilled
Oranges	2, squeezed for juice
Lime	1, squeezed for juice
Passion fruit	2, pulp and seeds
Pineapple	1 small, peeled, cored and grated
Sugar	to taste

Method

- Combine chilled tea with orange juice, lime juice and passion fruit pulp and seeds in a punch bowl.

- Add pineapple and sugar and stir until sugar dissolves.

- Pour into serving glasses and serve chilled.

POMEGRANATE DRINK

Makes about 2 litres (64 fl oz / 8 cups)

Ingredients

Pomegranates	5
Sugar	200 g (7 oz)
Lemon juice	2 Tbsp

Method

- Halve pomegranates and remove seeds. Reserve 4 Tbsp seeds for garnishing. Squeeze remaining seeds for juice using a fruit juice extractor or squeeze with hands through a muslin cloth. Strain and measure 500 ml (16 fl oz / 2 cups) juice.

- Pour juice, sugar and lemon juice into a small saucepan. Bring liquid to the boil over low heat, stirring constantly until sugar dissolves. Remove from heat and allow liquid to cool.

- Refrigerate until ready to serve. Pour into glasses and and add reserved pomegranate seeds before serving.

LAMB STOCK

Makes about 2 litres (64 fl oz / 8 cups)

Ingredients

Lamb	300 g (10^1/$_2$ oz), cut into chunks
Lamb bones	500 g (1 lb 1^1/$_2$ oz)
Red lentils	50 g (2 oz)
Onions	2, peeled and chopped
Garlic	2 cloves, peeled and crushed
Bay leaves	2
Red chillies	2, bruised
Ground turmeric	^{1}/$_2$ tsp
Water	3 litres (12 cups / 5^4/$_5$ pints)
Salt	to taste

Method

- Combine ingredients in a stock pot and bring to the boil. Simmer for 2 hours, skimming off froth as it surfaces. Strain.

- If not using stock immediately, set aside cool completely. When stock is cool, store in a freezer-safe container, cover and refrigerate for up to a week or freeze for up to 3 months.

WEIGHTS & MEASUREMENTS

Quantities for this book are given in Metric and American (spoon and cup) measures. Standard spoon and cup measurements used are: 1 tsp = 5 ml, 1 Tbsp = 15 ml, 1 cup = 250 ml. All measures are level unless otherwise stated.

LIQUID AND VOLUME MEASURES

Metric	Imperial	American
5 ml	$^1/_6$ fl oz	1 teaspoon
10 ml	$^1/_3$ fl oz	1 dessertspoon
15 ml	$^1/_2$ fl oz	1 tablespoon
60 ml	2 fl oz	$^1/_4$ cup (4 tablespoons)
85 ml	$2^1/_2$ fl oz	$^1/_3$ cup
90 ml	3 fl oz	$^3/_8$ cup (6 tablespoons)
125 ml	4 fl oz	$^1/_2$ cup
180 ml	6 fl oz	$^3/_4$ cup
250 ml	8 fl oz	1 cup
300 ml	10 fl oz ($^1/_2$ pint)	$1^1/_4$ cups
375 ml	12 fl oz	$1^1/_2$ cups
435 ml	14 fl oz	$1^3/_4$ cups
500 ml	16 fl oz	2 cups
625 ml	20 fl oz (1 pint)	$2^1/_2$ cups
750 ml	24 fl oz ($1^1/_5$ pints)	3 cups
1 litre	32 fl oz ($1^3/_5$ pints)	4 cups
1.25 litres	40 fl oz (2 pints)	5 cups
1.5 litres	48 fl oz ($2^2/_5$ pints)	6 cups
2.5 litres	80 fl oz (4 pints)	10 cups

DRY MEASURES

Metric	Imperial
30 grams	1 ounce
45 grams	$1^1/_2$ ounces
55 grams	2 ounces
70 grams	$2^1/_2$ ounces
85 grams	3 ounces
100 grams	$3^1/_2$ ounces
110 grams	4 ounces
125 grams	$4^1/_2$ ounces
140 grams	5 ounces
280 grams	10 ounces
450 grams	16 ounces (1 pound)
500 grams	1 pound, $1^1/_2$ ounces
700 grams	$1^1/_2$ pounds
800 grams	$1^3/_4$ pounds
1 kilogram	2 pounds, 3 ounces
1.5 kilograms	3 pounds, $4^1/_2$ ounces
2 kilograms	4 pounds, 6 ounces

LENGTH

Metric	Imperial
0.5 cm	$^1/_4$ inch
1 cm	$^1/_2$ inch
1.5 cm	$^3/_4$ inch
2.5 cm	1 inch

OVEN TEMPERATURE

	°C	°F	Gas Regulo
Very slow	120	250	1
Slow	150	300	2
Moderately slow	160	325	3
Moderate	180	350	4
Moderately hot	190/200	370/400	5/6
Hot	210/220	410/440	6/7
Very hot	230	450	8
Super hot	250/290	475/550	9/10

ABBREVIATION

tsp	teaspoon
Tbsp	tablespoon
g	gram
kg	kilogram
ml	millilitre